PHOENIX
SUNS

by Andres Ybarra

Published by ABDO Publishing Company, 8000 West 78th Street, Edina, Minnesota 55439. Copyright © 2012 by Abdo Consulting Group, Inc. International copyrights reserved in all countries. No part of this book may be reproduced in any form without written permission from the publisher. SportsZone™ is a trademark and logo of ABDO Publishing Company.

Printed in the United States of America,
North Mankato, Minnesota
062011
092011

♻ THIS BOOK CONTAINS AT LEAST 10% RECYCLED MATERIALS.

Editor: Dave McMahon
Copy Editor: Anna Comstock
Series design: Christa Schneider
Cover production: Marie Tupy
Interior production: Carol Castro

Photo Credits: Matt York/AP Images, cover, 44; Roberto Borea/AP Images, 1, 43 (top); Jeff Robbins/AP Images, 4, 32; Mark Elias/AP Images, 7, 8, 43 (middle); Focus on Sport/Getty Images, 10; Tom Hood/AP Images, 13; RBK/AP Images, 14, 42 (top); AP Images, 16; Rusty Kennedy/AP Images, 19, 20, 42 (middle); Jack Smith/AP Images, 22; Jeff Kida/AP Images, 25; Rick Stewart/Getty Images, 27, 42 (bottom); Bill Chan/AP Images, 28; Charles Bennett/AP Images, 31; Fred Jewell/AP Images, 34; Paul Connors/AP Images, 36; David Zalubowski/AP Images, 39; Rick Scuteri/AP Images, 40, 43 (bottom); Christian Petersen/Getty Images, 47

Library of Congress Cataloging-in-Publication Data
Ybarra, Andres, 1978-
 Phoenix Suns / by Andres Ybarra.
   p. cm. -- (Inside the NBA)
 ISBN 978-1-61783-172-0
 1. Phoenix Suns (Basketball team)--History--Juvenile literature. I. Title.
 GV885.22.P47Y32 2011
 796.323'640979173--dc23
                 2011020546

TABLE OF CONTENTS

CHAPTER 1

THE ALMOST VICTORY PARADE

Standing in uncomfortably hot temperatures and waiting for hours just to watch a parade does not sound very appealing. But that is exactly what hundreds of thousands of people did in sweltering downtown Phoenix, Arizona, on June 26, 1993.

The people were there to cheer on the Phoenix Suns as they paraded in cars down the streets. The Suns had just completed their National Basketball Association (NBA) Finals series against the Chicago Bulls. It was the hottest day of the year up to that point, but the people were there to show their support. And the Suns did not even win the title.

That was how much the Phoenix fans respected their team. The Suns had lost Game 6 of the 1993 Finals to Michael Jordan and the Chicago Bulls six days earlier. But that did not matter. A crowd of 300,000 stretched more than two miles

The Suns' Charles Barkley returns to the bench after the Bulls' John Paxson hit a three-point shot to win the 1993 NBA Finals.

THE "ROUND MOUND OF REBOUND"

Charles Barkley is one of the most successful and colorful figures in NBA history. Barkley, a forward, played in more than 1,000 games over 16 NBA seasons. He averaged 22.1 points per game for his career. A former league Most Valuable Player (MVP), Barkley was inducted into the Basketball Hall of Fame in 2006.

But he is also equally known for his wild ways. With nicknames like "The Chuckster," "Sir Charles," and "The Round Mound of Rebound," Barkley had a way with words. "I don't create controversies. They're there long before I open my mouth. I just bring them to your attention," he once said.

Much like the Suns, though, Barkley had a career full of success but never won an NBA title.

(3.2 km) through downtown to celebrate the team's season.

The fans became so crazy that police actually had to remove star player Charles Barkley from the parade. The parade had not yet moved two blocks, but so many people were running up to his car that he had to leave. Barkley later waved to the crowd from a safer place after the parade.

Nearly 780,000 total fans had watched the team play that season. That was a team record for attendance. At the season's end, Phoenix led the NBA in scoring and finished with the league's best record at 62–20. In the playoffs, the Suns trailed the Los Angeles Lakers two games to none in the first round. The Suns then won three games in a row to take the series. They then went on to beat the San Antonio Spurs and Seattle

From left, Charles Barkley, Kevin Johnson, and Danny Ainge celebrate in the third overtime of their 129–121 win over the Chicago Bulls in the 1993 Finals. Tom Chambers, *rear left*, and Dan Majerle also join them.

SuperSonics to reach the championship round.

In the Finals, the Suns gave the defending NBA champion Bulls a good fight. The first team to win four games would win the series. Chicago won the first two games in Phoenix.

But Phoenix then won two of the following three games on Chicago's home court. Game 3 was perhaps the most exciting of those wins, as it took three overtimes for Phoenix to win.

The series then returned to Phoenix for Game 6 with the Suns trailing three games to two. With a late lead and a loud Phoenix crowd behind them, the Suns seemed destined to

The Suns' Kevin Johnson chases a loose ball while being trailed by the Bulls' Michael Jordan during the 1993 NBA Finals.

force a Game 7. But then Chicago's John Paxson sank a three-pointer with less than four seconds to play in the fourth quarter. That gave the Bulls a one-point victory. The Bulls had won their third NBA title in three years.

With a single shot, one of the best seasons in Suns history had come to an end. It was the second time in team history that the Suns had lost in the NBA Finals.

So there was no victory lap around the downtown Phoenix streets. And there was no championship trophy. Instead, the 1992–93 Suns and their fans had to settle for a runners-up parade. Through the 2010–11 season, the Suns still had not made it back to the Finals since that dream run in 1993.

Championship or not, though, the Suns have been successful in the NBA. Phoenix has been home to such star players as Barkley, forward Connie Hawkins, guard Kevin Johnson, guard Steve Nash, and forward Amar'e Stoudemire.

Phoenix coaches John MacLeod and Cotton Fitzsimmons also set high standards. They combined to win more than 900 games over three decades, beginning in the 1970s. And the NBA would not be what it is today without Jerry Colangelo, the Suns' chairman and previous owner who helped the NBA grow in popularity.

The Suns' players, coaches, and executives have all worked to make Phoenix one of the most successful teams in NBA history. In fact, only three teams had better all-time winning

Jerry Colangelo

Jerry Colangelo was the first general manager of the Suns dating back to their start in 1968. He remained with the team for more than four decades. Through 2010–11, no other team executive in NBA history had stayed that long with a single team. Colangelo, who was inducted into the Basketball Hall of Fame in 2004, was also one of the masterminds at USA Basketball. USA Basketball organizes the United States' participation in the Olympics. Colangelo helped build the Team USA squad that won the gold medal at the 2008 Olympic Games. It was the first Olympic gold medal for Team USA since 2000.

percentages than the Suns through the 2009–10 season. Those teams are the Los Angeles Lakers, the San Antonio Spurs, and the Boston Celtics. However, they all had won several NBA titles. The Suns, on the other hand, always seemed to come up short of a title. Still, Phoenix remains one of the most storied teams in the league.

CHAPTER 2

THE NBA RISES IN THE DESERT

When the Phoenix Suns joined the NBA in the late 1960s, most of the teams in the league were from the East and West Coasts.

Cities such as New York, Philadelphia, Boston, Atlanta, Los Angeles, Seattle, and San Francisco already had NBA teams. Teams in Chicago, Detroit, and Cincinnati represented the Midwest in the NBA.

Arizona and Arizona State had major college sports teams. But until 1968, no professional sports team of any kind had been started in the Arizona desert. Some thought that Phoenix was too small, too hot, and too far away from the rest of the major cities that had professional teams to successfully host its own.

But all of that changed when a group of businessmen decided they wanted to have an NBA team in Phoenix. Richard Bloch led the group and worked hard to bring a team to the city.

"The Original Sun" Dick Van Arsdale (5) played for the Suns from 1968 to 1977. He scored the first points in team history in 1968.

In January 1968, Bloch received word that the NBA had approved the creation of a new team for Phoenix. It was one of two teams that would join the league in the 1968–69 season. The Milwaukee Bucks were the other. So Bloch had a team, and he also had an arena called Veterans Memorial Coliseum. The arena was located at the Arizona State Fairgrounds. It would house Phoenix's new NBA team. All that was left to find were some players, a coach, and a general manager.

The ownership group, guided by Bloch, chose Jerry Colangelo as the team's general manager. Colangelo had been a scout and assistant coach with the Chicago Bulls. He also had been a basketball player in college at Illinois. Colangelo was just 28 years old at the time, making him the youngest general manager in league history.

Colangelo then selected Johnny "Red" Kerr as the team's coach. And the Suns got their first player when they selected guard/forward Dick Van Arsdale on May 6, 1968, in the NBA Expansion Draft. Van Arsdale would become known as "The Original Sun."

In addition to being the team's first player, Van Arsdale had another important first in Suns history, as well. He scored

Jerry Colangelo, *left*, shown with Steve Nash in 2005, was the Suns' general manager in their inaugural season in 1968–69.

the team's first points when he made a layup against the Seattle SuperSonics in the Suns' first game on October 16, 1968. In front of 7,000 fans at Veterans Memorial Coliseum, the Suns defeated the SuperSonics 116–107. It was one of only a small number of wins the Suns would post in their first season. Phoenix finished the year with a 16–66 record and in last place in the Western Division.

Van Arsdale went on to become a three-time NBA All-Star. After his playing days were over, Van Arsdale spent a half season as interim head coach. He eventually became an executive for the Suns.

"I've never had any desire to go anywhere else," Van Arsdale said in 2001. "My wife and I love the Southwest, and it's a great feeling to know [you're] wanted and that you can still

The Suns' Connie Hawkins (42) uses his long reach to shoot past Billy Cunningham (32) of the Philadelphia 76ers in 1969.

contribute to the organization. And whatever happens, it's been a good run."

Phoenix started making some progress in the league during the 1969–70 season. The Suns had won the coin flip to secure the rights to American Basketball Association (ABA) star Connie Hawkins. "The

A Logo is Born

The Suns originally paid an artist $5,000 to create their first logo back in 1968. But team officials did not like it. Instead, they charged Stan Fabe, a Tucson resident who operated a commercial printing plant, with the task. For only $200, Fabe designed the Suns' famous sunburst logo. The logo eventually changed over time, but it kept many similarities with Fabe's creation.

Hawk," as he came to be known, would go on to become one of the most exciting players in NBA history. He helped bring the Suns more publicity, too. Hawkins led the team in scoring at 24.6 points per game. He also played in the NBA All-Star Game.

With Hawkins leading the way, Phoenix ended its second season at 39–43. That record was good enough to qualify for the postseason that year. In their first-ever playoff series, the Suns took the Los Angeles Lakers to seven games. But the Lakers, led by Wilt Chamberlain, pounded Phoenix by 35 points in Game 7 to win the series.

It was a difficult end to the season. But playing in the postseason became one of the team's hallmarks.

LOSING OUT ON KAREEM

In their inaugural 1968–69 season, the Suns finished with the worst record in the NBA and in last place in the Western Division. The last-place team in the Eastern Division was the Milwaukee Bucks. To determine who would pick first in the upcoming NBA Draft, the teams had to flip a coin. The Bucks won the coin flip, and they drafted Lew Alcindor from the University of California, Los Angeles. Two years later, the future Hall of Famer led the Bucks to an NBA title. After that season, Alcindor changed his name to Kareem Abdul-Jabbar.

The Suns got another chance at an important coin flip two months later. The Suns and Seattle Super-Sonics were given the chance to flip a coin for the rights to American Basketball Association star Connie Hawkins. This time the Suns won. "The Hawk" eventually became enshrined in the Hall of Fame.

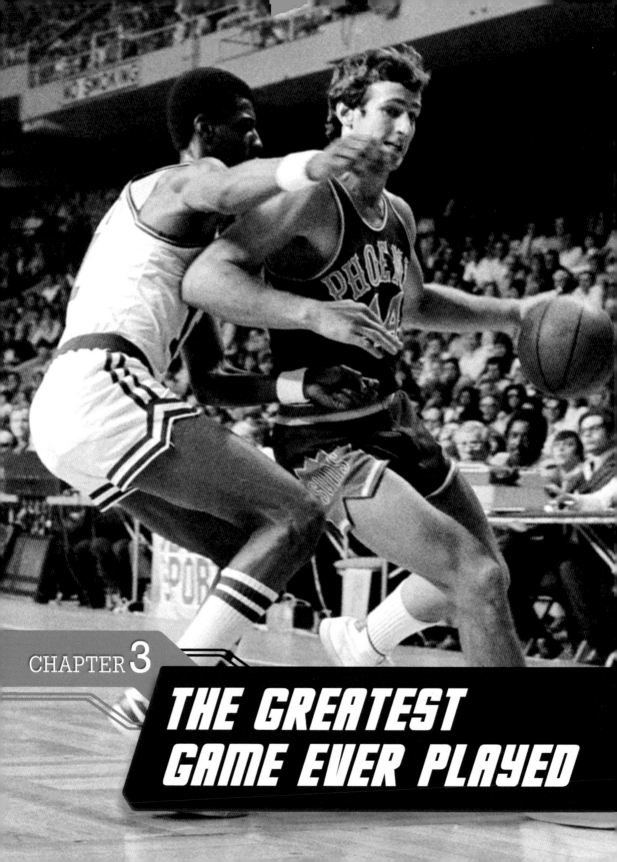

CHAPTER 3

THE GREATEST GAME EVER PLAYED

Of all the NBA games ever played, it is nearly impossible to pick one as the greatest ever played. But many of the people who watched Game 5 of the 1976 NBA Finals are convinced they saw it.

"After all these years, the thing that occurs to me is what a privilege it is to have been involved in that game," former Suns guard Paul Westphal said in 2001. "That game meant so much to so many people. It's a game that nearly every fan who watched still remembers."

After failing to qualify for the playoffs the previous five seasons, the Suns returned to the postseason during the 1975–76 season under coach John MacLeod. Westphal and center Alvan Adams were strong additions to the team, but the Suns still struggled. At

The Suns' Paul Westphal dribbles past the Celtics' Charlie Scott during the 1976 NBA Finals at the Boston Garden. Westphal helped the team come back from last place in their division to reach the Finals.

The John MacLeod Era

Cotton Fitzsimmons is probably the most recognizable coach in Suns history. But the man who guided the team for more than 13 seasons in the club's early days was John MacLeod. On March 30, 1973, MacLeod became the fifth head coach in the Suns' brief history. But seven days before that, MacLeod made a strong impression on the team. He had been invited into the locker room to diagram a few plays before a game against the Golden State Warriors. General manager Jerry Colangelo was obviously impressed. He offered MacLeod the coaching job. The Suns would go on to win 579 games under MacLeod.

one point, there was a stretch during which they went 4–18. That sank the Suns to last place in their division. They had also lost star player Dick Van Arsdale to a broken wrist.

Even so, Phoenix rallied to finish the season with a 42–40 record. The Suns knocked out the Seattle SuperSonics in the first round of the postseason.

Next, they upset the defending champion Golden State Warriors to earn their first trip to the NBA Finals. In the Finals, the Suns faced the Boston Celtics. The Celtics had already won 12 NBA titles. Phoenix helped the Celtics write one of the most exciting chapters in Boston's rich history.

The Celtics were led by two of the game's all-time stars, Dave Cowens and John Havlicek. The Celtics won the first two games of the series and seemed to be on their way to their 13th world title. But Phoenix surprised the Celtics with two straight wins at Veterans Memorial Coliseum. And that set the stage for what would become known as "The Greatest Game Ever Played."

Game 5 was played at the historic Boston Garden. Suns forward Keith Erickson sprained his ankle when he

Suns center Alvan Adams, shown going up for a shot against the Philadelphia 76ers in 1976, helped the Suns reach the Finals that year.

A Hostile Garden

In Game 5 of the 1976 NBA Finals, Celtics fans at the Boston Garden got a little too excited after the home team appeared to win at the end of the second overtime. A crowd of fans ran onto the court in celebration, but referee Richie Powers ruled there was still one second left on the clock. The Celtics fans were not too happy. One was so upset that he punched Powers in the face.

stepped on Havlicek's foot early in the game. That helped the Celtics jump out to an early lead, and they stayed ahead for nearly the entire game.

But the Suns came back. Phoenix finally took the lead with only 23 seconds left to play in the fourth quarter. Havlicek then hit two free throws to send

The Suns' Garfield Heard (24) handles a rebound against the Philadelphia 76ers' George McGinnis in 1976.

the game into the first of three overtime sessions.

The first overtime provided the most memorable moment of the game. Boston's Paul Silas tried to call a timeout with three seconds left and the game tied at 101–101. But Boston was out of timeouts. That violation should have resulted in a technical foul and a free throw for the Suns. However, referee Richie Powers did not make the call, and the game was sent into a second overtime.

With the second overtime came another tough call by Powers. Havlicek appeared to give

The Ring of Honor

The Suns have a "Ring of Honor" to recognize their top players and team officials. As of 2011, there were 12 members. The members include Alvan Adams, Charles Barkley, Tom Chambers, Jerry Colangelo, Walter Davis, Cotton Fitzsimmons, Connie Hawkins, Kevin Johnson, Dan Majerle, Joe Proski, Dick Van Arsdale, and Paul Westphal. Of the 12 men, only Colangelo, Fitzsimmons, and Proski are not former Suns players. Colangelo was the team's first general manager. Fitzsimmons was a coach, and Proski was the team's trainer for 32 years.

Phoenix's Garfield Heard sank an 18-foot jump shot to send the game to a third overtime.

Both teams were tired, but the Celtics eventually held on to win 128–126. Westphal and guard Ricky Sobers scored 25 points apiece for the Suns. Teammate Curtis Perry, a 6-foot-7 forward, scored 23 points and had 15 rebounds. Adams scored 20 points, and Heard finished with 17 points and 12 rebounds.

The Celtics ended the series by beating the Suns 87–80 in Game 6. Phoenix went on to finish with winning records in six of its next eight seasons. The Suns made seven playoff appearances during that stretch, including two trips to the Western Conference finals.

the Celtics a one-point victory with a running jump shot as time ran out. Powers, however, said that exactly one second was left on the clock after the shot. That gave Phoenix enough time to commit a technical foul, which gave the Celtics a free throw. The Suns then had an opportunity to bring the ball in at midcourt, which gave them their best chance to score and tie the game. The plan worked.

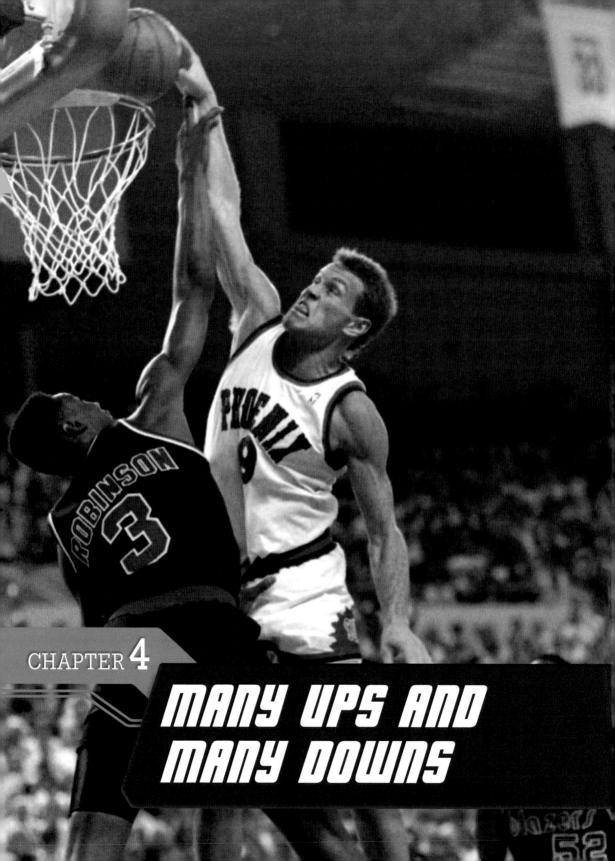

CHAPTER 4

MANY UPS AND MANY DOWNS

Phoenix advanced to the NBA playoffs because they were steady. The Suns' post-season performances, however, were not quite as reliable.

Phoenix's 1983–84 season ended with a last-second miss against the Los Angeles Lakers during the Western Conference finals in 1984. That marked the beginning of several disappointing years for the Suns.

In 1984, Phoenix began the first of four consecutive losing seasons. However, they still managed to qualify for the playoffs in 1984–85 with a 36–46 record. The Lakers swept them in three games in the first round of the postseason. The next year, Phoenix went winless in its first nine games. The Suns never fully recovered, and they finished the season 32–50. That was the most losses that they had endured since the 1974–75 season.

The Suns' Dan Majerle goes in for a dunk against Cliff Robinson of the Portland Trail Blazers during the 1990 NBA playoffs in Phoenix.

TOM CHAMBERS

An unrestricted free agent is a player whose contract with his team has expired. The player is free to sign with any team. The first-ever unrestricted free agent in the NBA was Tom Chambers. Nicknamed "TC" and "Tommy Gun," Chambers signed with the Suns in 1988. He had played the previous five seasons with the Seattle SuperSonics.

In Chambers five seasons in Phoenix, the Suns went to the Western Conference finals three times. They also went to the NBA Finals once. His 60-point game against the Sonics is the best single-game scoring effort in Suns history.

In the 1989–90 season, his second with Phoenix, Chambers averaged 27.2 points per game. Chambers scored nearly 9,000 points as a Sun, counting both the regular season and playoffs.

The Suns' struggles continued into the 1986–87 season. Coach John MacLeod was fired in February 1987. MacLeod had been the Suns' coach for more than 13 years, but the team's poor performance called for a change. Dick Van Arsdale, "The Original Sun," took over as coach for the rest of the season. He had retired as a player for the Suns a decade earlier. The Suns finished the season 14–12 over its last 26 games with Van Arsdale as coach.

The Suns went 28–54 in the 1987–88 season under another new coach, John Wetzel. That was their worst record since their first year in the league. Surprisingly, however, the Suns followed that poor showing with the third-biggest turnaround in NBA history after they let Wetzel go.

Tom Chambers (24) tries to get past the defense of Utah's Karl Malone during the 1990 playoffs in Phoenix.

Under coach Cotton Fitzsimmons, the Suns finished 55–27 in the 1988–89 season and returned to the NBA playoffs. This time, the team included all-time greats like Tom Chambers, Kevin Johnson, Dan Majerle, and Jeff Hornacek. That group led the team to two consecutive trips to the Western Conference finals. The first appearance resulted in a four-game sweep by the Lakers.

The following year, however, the Suns had a stronger showing. They finished the season with only one win fewer than the previous campaign. But Phoenix averaged 114 points per game that season, which ranked second in the NBA. The Suns also set team records for road wins (22), consecutive home wins (19), and

Cotton Fitzsimmons

Lowell "Cotton" Fitzsimmons had three separate stints as the Suns' head coach. The first was from 1970 to 1972. He became the coach again from 1988 to 1992. And in 1996, he once again took over, replacing coach Paul Westphal. During the 1996–97 season, Fitzsimmons was replaced by Danny Ainge. All told, Fitzsimmons won 341 games as the Suns' head coach, with 208 losses. During his career, he also had coaching stints with the Atlanta Hawks, the Buffalo Braves, the Kansas City Kings, and the San Antonio Spurs.

sellouts (26). Individually, Chambers set a club record for points in a season (2,201) and scoring average (27.2).

More important, though, was the fact that the Suns finally beat the Lakers in a seven-game playoff series. After being swept a year earlier, Phoenix eliminated the Lakers in the 1990 Western Conference semifinals. But the Suns still fell short of reaching the NBA Finals. They lost four games to two to the Portland Trail Blazers in the conference finals.

By this time, Phoenix had become known as an offensive power because of their high-scoring players. The Suns would go on to win 108 total games over the next two seasons. On November 10, 1990, Fitzsimmons became only the seventh coach in NBA history to win 700 games. As a team, the Suns also set an NBA record with 107 first-half points and 173 total points against Denver on November 10, 1990. They became the 12th NBA team to win 1,000 games, and they sold out all 41 home games during the 1990-91 season.

But despite all of those successes, the Suns could not end their playoff troubles. In 1991, they lost in four games to the Utah Jazz in the opening

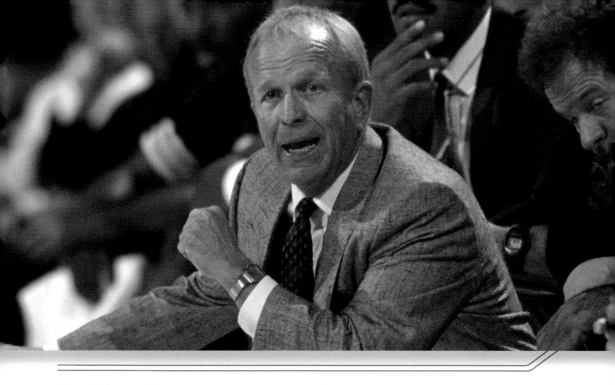

Coach Cotton Fitzsimmons was a familiar face to Suns fans. He coached the team three different times and won a total of 341 games.

round. In 1992, the Portland Trail Blazers beat them in five games in the second round.

The Suns were reliable about making the postseason, but they still were not quite strong enough to make a serious run at the NBA title. Along the way, the Suns had not had a superstar since Connie Hawkins. But that was about to change as the Suns headed into their 25th season.

Lakers Rivalry

The Suns have often found themselves on the losing side of their long rivalry with the Los Angeles Lakers. In fact, the Lakers defeated the Suns the first six times the two teams met in the playoffs. Phoenix finally won a series in 1990. After the Lakers won the 2010 Western Conference finals against the Suns, Los Angeles had an all-time playoff record against Phoenix of 8–4.

CHAPTER 5

A SECOND CHANCE

By 1992, Charles Barkley had become one of the NBA's most popular players. The 6-foot-6 power forward for the Philadelphia 76ers was one of the most dominant rebounders of his era. He was also one of the most controversial players of his time.

Nicknamed "Sir Charles," Barkley was just as well known for his bad behavior on and off the court as he was for his excellent basketball skills.

On June 17, 1992, Barkley was traded to Phoenix for Jeff Hornacek, Andrew Lang, and Tim Perry. It was perhaps the biggest move the Suns had made since they had won the rights to Connie Hawkins in 1969. Barkley's arrival immediately energized the team. He gave the Suns a star player who could dominate a game. The Suns had a new home at America West Arena, as well

Charles Barkley, shown shooting in 1993, helped the Suns post a 62–20 record in the 1992–93 season. That was the best record in the league.

as new uniforms. And former Suns great Paul Westphal was taking over as coach.

The Suns became one of the clear early favorites for the NBA crown. Barkley led the way up front. Kevin Johnson ran the offense in the backcourt. And "Thunder" Dan Majerle became one of the most dangerous three-point shooters in the game.

The Suns tied the NBA's third-best record for a month by going 14–0 in December (other teams have gone unbeaten in more games during that month). Barkley and Majerle represented the Suns at the NBA All-Star Game. As a team, Phoenix broke the NBA record for three-pointers made in a single season with 398. And their average of 113.4 points per game led the league. Barkley averaged 25.6 points and 12.2 rebounds per game on his

"Thunder Dan"

Dan Majerle originally earned the nickname "Thunder Dan" in his early days in the league. He was known for his rough inside play and "thunderous" dunks. Eventually, however, Majerle became better known as a long-range shooting threat. He was the team's all-time leader in three-point field goals with 800 until Steve Nash broke his record in 2009. Majerle played seven seasons for the Suns, spent one year with the Cleveland Cavaliers, and then played five seasons for the Miami Heat. He returned to Phoenix for the final year of his career and retired as a player before becoming an assistant coach for the Suns.

way to becoming the first Suns player to be named the NBA's MVP. General manager Jerry Colangelo became the first person to be named the NBA's Executive of the Year for a fourth time.

And most importantly, Phoenix finished with a 62–20 record. That was the best in the NBA. In the first round of the

Dan Majerle, *right*, drives past the Bulls' Michael Jordan in Game 3 of the 1993 NBA Finals. Majerle made six three-point shots in the game.

playoffs, the Suns faced their old rival, the Los Angeles Lakers. The Lakers shocked the Suns by winning the first two games of the five-game series in Phoenix. Following the Game 2 loss, though, Westphal made a bold prediction. He said, "We're going to win the series."

The Suns rallied and became the first team to come back from a two-games-to-none playoff deficit. They won the series three games to two. In Game 5, Barkley had 31 points and 14 rebounds. Kevin Johnson added 24 points and 13 assists. And the Suns' Oliver

Suns guard Kevin Johnson, shown going up for a shot in 1990, had his jersey number—No. 7—retired in 2001.

Miller also had a big game with 17 points and 14 rebounds.

The San Antonio Spurs were up next. The Spurs had defeated the defending conference champion Portland Trail Blazers in the first round. But the Suns defeated the Spurs in six games. They then began a series against the Seattle SuperSonics. The teams traded win after win. It took 44 points and 24 rebounds from Barkley for the Suns to defeat the Sonics 123–110 in Game 7. Kevin Johnson scored 22 points and Chambers had 17 for the Suns. And after 17 years, the Phoenix Suns had earned a return trip to the NBA Finals.

Like their first time in the Finals, however, the Suns were up against one of the strongest teams in league history. Michael Jordan's Chicago Bulls were looking to win their third title in a row. They had won titles the previous two seasons against the Lakers and the Trail Blazers.

As they had in the opening round against the Lakers, the Suns fell into an early hole against the Bulls. They trailed two games to none but came back to win two of the next three games. That set up Game 6 back in Phoenix. Ultimately, the Suns and the Bulls scored the same number of points (640) over the whole series. But in the end, it came down to a single play.

With Phoenix leading 98–96 and 14.1 seconds remaining in the game,

KJ, MR. MAYOR

The Suns retired Kevin Johnson's jersey number—No. 7—in 2001, when he joined the team's "Ring of Honor" as one of the best players in team history. The 6-foot-1-inch guard, nicknamed "KJ," became known for his quickness during his parts of 12 seasons in Phoenix.

He was a three-time All-Star, and as of 2011, he held the Suns' career records for assists (6,518), free throws made (3,851), and free throws attempted (4,579).

During the 1988–89 season, Johnson joined Hall of Famers Isiah Thomas and Magic Johnson as one of three players in NBA history to have averaged at least 20 points and 12 assists per game in a season. In 2008, Johnson became mayor of his hometown, Sacramento, California.

Jordan brought the ball up the court. Everyone expected him to take the final shot, but he passed the ball to Scottie Pippen. Pippen drove toward the basket, where he dumped the ball off to forward Horace Grant. Grant had been struggling all game. So rather than take the shot, he passed the ball back out. John Paxson was waiting at the three-point line.

Paxson buried the three-pointer. With 3.9 seconds left, Phoenix had one last chance. Johnson drove the foul line area, but his shot was swatted away, leaving Chicago with its third NBA title. Barkley and the Suns walked off the court dejected while the Bulls celebrated on the America West Arena floor. Barkley and Majerle scored 21 points apiece and Johnson had 19, but it was not enough.

The Suns returned to the playoffs the following two seasons, but lost both times to the eventual champion Houston Rockets. As it was so many times in the past, the Suns were so close to the world title only to fall a couple of plays short.

The Suns' Danny Ainge, *left*, and Dan Majerle take a break on the bench during Game 4 of the 1993 NBA Finals.

CHAPTER 6

PERENNIAL CONTENDERS

Since their appearance in the 1993 NBA Finals, the Suns had continued success. They advanced to the Western Conference finals in 2005, 2006, and 2010. Suns fans watched two of the greatest point guards of their era, Jason Kidd and Steve Nash, run the team's offense.

Forwards Shawn Marion and Amar'e Stoudemire threw down slam dunks. And Marion and Stephon Marbury became the team's first All-Star pairing since Charles Barkley and Dan Majerle. Stoudemire was named Rookie of the Year in 2003. And Nash won MVP Awards in 2005 and 2006. Even superstar center Shaquille O'Neal made a brief stop to play in Phoenix for two seasons. He represented the Suns in the NBA All-Star Game and was named co-MVP of the game in 2009 with Lakers star Kobe Bryant.

Heading into the 1996–97 season, the Suns made a series of moves that would change

Forward Amar'e Stoudemire won the Rookie of the Year Award in 2003 and went on to an All-Star career with the Suns.

AMAR'E STOUDEMIRE

Amar'e Stoudemire did not start playing organized basketball until he was 14, but it did not take long for him to develop his amazing talents. The Suns drafted the 6-foot-10 power forward straight out of high school in 2002, and an All-Star career was born. It was not trouble-free, however. Two separate knee injuries forced Stoudemire to miss most of the 2005–06 season. He came back the following season, though, and was the only player to play in all 82 games. During the 2007–08 season, Stoudemire became the first player since San Antonio's Tim Duncan in 2001–02 to average 25 points, nine rebounds, and two blocks per game for a season. Stoudemire spent the first eight years of his career with the Suns. He then signed with the New York Knicks in 2010.

the face of the team for years to come. They traded Barkley to the Houston Rockets and acquired Kidd from the Dallas Mavericks. They also drafted Nash that year and named Danny Ainge as their head coach nine games into the season. It would be several years before Nash would develop into an All-Star point guard.

After going 40–42 in 1996–97, the Suns returned to their winning ways. This time, Kidd led the way. Forwards Danny Manning, George McCloud, and Tom Gugliotta also contributed. During the Kidd era, the Suns advanced to the playoffs five times, but lost in the opening round in four of those series.

In 2000, the Suns had advanced to the Western Conference semifinals, but lost in five games to the Los Angeles Lakers. After another

Suns guard Jason Kidd, *right,* led the Suns to the playoffs five times before he was traded to the New Jersey Nets.

first-round exit from the play-offs, Kidd was traded in July 2001 to the New Jersey Nets for Marbury. It was one of many trades the Suns made that year in another effort to make them better.

The Suns missed the play-offs for two out of the next three seasons. But players like Marbury, Marion, and former All-Star Anfernee "Penny" Hardaway were on the team, so they had talent to build around. Stoudemire also was drafted in 2002.

Phoenix got back on track during the 2004–05 season, when Nash returned to the Suns as a free agent. The start-ing five of Nash, Stoudemire, Marion, Joe Johnson, and

Steve Nash won consecutive league MVP Awards in 2005 and 2006.

Steve Nash

After returning to Phoenix for the 2004–05 season, Steve Nash became the face of the Suns. Originally drafted by the team in 1996, Nash was the second player in Suns history to be named the NBA's MVP. He was the first point guard since Lakers great Magic Johnson in 1990 to win the honor. He was also the first Canadian player to receive the award. Nash was named MVP again the following season.

Quentin Richardson was one of the best in the league. The Suns actually matched their 1992–93 season record of 62–20. That allowed them to earn the top seed in the playoffs in 2005.

Nash won the first of his two MVP Awards that season, and Mike D'Antoni was named Coach of the Year in only his second season with the team. The

Suns made it all the way to the Western Conference finals, but lost in five games to the eventual champion, the San Antonio Spurs. The next season, they lost again in the conference finals. This time, the Suns lost to the Dallas Mavericks.

The Suns did not return to the conference championship round until 2010. Many considered the 2010 postseason to be the Suns' best chance to return to the NBA Finals, and they almost did. But in the Conference finals the Suns ran into Bryant and the defending champion Lakers.

Los Angeles won the first two games before the Suns responded with a pair of wins to tie the series. After the Lakers won Game 5 103–101, they won the series with a 111–103 victory in Game 6. Stoudemire led the Suns in Game 6 with 27 points, followed by Nash with 21 and 13 from Jason Richardson.

After the 2009–10 season, Stoudemire left the Suns as a free agent. In his absence, Phoenix struggled to finish 40–42 in 2010–11, missing the playoffs for the second time in three years. However, backed by veterans such as Nash, Vince Carter, and Grant Hill, the Suns continue to give fans hope for a future championship.

Grant Hill

Grant Hill's NBA career has been solid, but injuries have slowed his progress. After putting up strong numbers in his first six seasons with the Detroit Pistons, Hill began having serious injuries. They forced him to miss 292 out of 492 games over his next six years in Orlando with the Magic. Hill got his career back on track when he signed with the Suns in 2007. He averaged 13.2 points per game in his first year in Phoenix. The following year, he played in all 82 games for the first time in his long career.

TIMELINE

1968 The NBA Board of Governors grants an expansion franchise to the city of Phoenix. The nickname "Suns" is selected in a contest sponsored by the Arizona Republic. Jerry Colangelo is named general manager at 28 years old.

1969 The team wins the rights to ABA star Connie Hawkins and proceeds to make its first playoff appearance despite having a losing record (39–43).

1976 The Suns clinch their first playoff berth in six years and advance to the NBA Finals, where they lose in six games to the Boston Celtics. The Sporting News names Colangelo NBA Executive of the Year and center Alvan Adams wins the NBA's Rookie of the Year honor. Hawkins becomes the first Suns player to have his number retired.

1987 Longtime head coach John MacLeod is released by the team after more than 13 seasons and replaced on the bench by Dick Van Arsdale.

1989 The Suns complete the third-biggest turnaround in NBA history by finishing 55–27. Eddie Johnson wins the NBA's Sixth Man Award. Kevin Johnson is named the NBA's Most Improved Player. Cotton Fitzsimmons takes the Coach of the Year honor. And Colangelo is named the NBA's Executive of the Year for the third time.

1990 The Suns defeat the Lakers for the first time in a seven-game playoff series after they win in five games in the Western Conference semifinals. The Suns lose to the Portland Trail Blazers in the conference finals. The following November, Fitzsimmons becomes the seventh coach in NBA history to win 700 career games.

1993	Led by Charles Barkley, the Suns finish an NBA-best 62–20 and secure the top seed in the NBA playoffs. They reach the NBA Finals for the second time in team history and lose to the Chicago Bulls in six games. Colangelo is named the NBA's Executive of the Year a fourth time.
1995	The Houston Rockets defeat the Suns for a second straight year in the playoffs en route to back-to-back NBA titles.
1996	Barkley becomes the 10th player in league history to reach 20,000 points and 10,000 rebounds. Michael Finley becomes the first Suns rookie since Walter Davis to score 1,000 points in his first season.
1998	Kevin Johnson moves past Nate "Tiny" Archibald into 10th place on the all-time NBA career assist list and scores his 13,000th career point.
2003	Marbury and Shawn Marion become the first Suns All-Star tandem since Barkley and Majerle in 1993. Amar'e Stoudemire wins the NBA's Rookie of the Year Award.
2005	Steve Nash is named the NBA's MVP, Mike D'Antoni is named the NBA's Coach of the Year, and Bryan Colangelo is named the NBA's Executive of the Year.
2006	Nash wins his second-straight MVP award, and the Suns advance to the Western Conference finals, losing to Dallas in six games. America West Arena is renamed US Airways Center.
2010	The Suns advance to the Western Conference finals, losing in six games to the eventual champion Los Angeles Lakers.

QUICK STATS

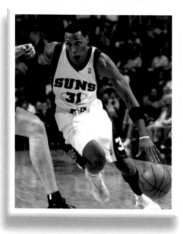

FRANCHISE HISTORY

Phoenix Suns (1968–)

NBA FINALS

1976, 1993

CONFERENCE FINALS

1976, 1979, 1984, 1989, 1990, 1993, 2005, 2006, 2010

DIVISION CHAMPIONSHIPS

1981, 1993, 1995, 2005, 2006, 2007

KEY PLAYERS
(position[s]; years with team)

Alvan Adams (F/C; 1975–88)
Charles Barkley (F; 1992–96)
Tom Chambers (F; 1988–93)
Walter Davis (G; 1977–88)

Connie Hawkins (F; 1969–74)
Jeff Hornacek (G; 1986–92)
Kevin Johnson (G; 1987–98, 2000)
Jason Kidd (G; 1996–2001)
Dan Majerle (G; 1988–1995,
    2001–02)
Shawn Marion (F; 1999–2008)
Steve Nash (G; 1996–98, 2004–)
Amar'e Stoudemire (F; 2002–10)
Dick Van Arsdale (G/F; 1968–77)
Mark West (C; 1988–94, 1999–2000)
Paul Westphal (G; 1975–80,
    1983–84)

KEY COACHES

Mike D'Antoni (2003–08):
    253–136; 26–25 (postseason)
Cotton Fitzsimmons (1970–72,
    1988–92, 1996):
    341–208; 22–22 (postseason)
John MacLeod (1973–87):
    579–543; 37–44 (postseason)
Paul Westphal (1992–96):
    191–88; 25–19 (postseason)

HOME ARENAS

Veterans Memorial Coliseum
    (1968–1992)
US Airways Center (2006–)
—Known as America West Arena
    (1993–2005)

* All statistics through 2010–11 season

QUOTES AND ANECDOTES

The date January 26, 1971, marked a historical moment for the Phoenix Suns. The Suns were hosting the visiting Buffalo Braves in Phoenix that night. However, the Braves' road uniforms did not make it to Phoenix in time for the game. Oddly enough, the Braves had their home uniforms, so the Suns wore their road uniforms at home. It was the only time the team wore road uniforms for a home game.

Charles Barkley was known for keeping things loose among teammates. One example came during the 1992–93 season when a game in Denver was delayed because the lights went out. To keep the mood light, Barkley and Dan Majerle found a football and started throwing touchdown passes. Not everybody (in particular, Denver's Dikembe Mutombo) found it amusing. But when the lights came back on, the Suns were ready for action. "We were ready to play, and they weren't," recalled coach Paul Westphal.

"So we're down 0–2, I know the next question is, 'Are you guys dead?' No, we're going to win the series. We're going to win one Tuesday. Then the next game's Thursday, we'll win there, and then we'll come back and we'll win the series on Sunday. Everybody will say what a great series it was." —Paul Westphal addressing the media after the Suns went down two games to none to the Los Angeles Lakers in the first round of the 1993 NBA playoffs. Phoenix went on to win the series in five games.

"There are a lot of great players and a lot of great coaches in the Hall of Fame, but nobody has contributed more to the game of basketball." —Cotton Fitzsimmons on Jerry Colangelo's induction into the Naismith Memorial Basketball Hall of Fame

GLOSSARY

archrival

The opponent that brings out the greatest emotion in a team, its fans, and its players.

backcourt

The point guards and shooting guards on a basketball team.

contender

A team that is in the race for a championship or playoff berth.

contract

A binding agreement about, for example, years of commitment by a basketball player in exchange for a given salary.

draft

A system used by professional sports leagues to select new players in order to spread incoming talent among all teams. The NBA Draft is held each June.

expansion

In sports, the addition of a franchise or franchises to a league.

free agent

A player whose contract has expired and who is able to sign with the team of his choice.

general manager

The executive who is in charge of the team's overall operation. He or she hires and fires coaches, drafts players, and signs free agents.

interim

Temporarily holding a position until a permanent replacement is found.

perennial

Happening every year.

postseason

The games in which the best teams play after the regular-season schedule has been completed.

rebound

To secure the basketball after a missed shot.

rookie

A first-year player in the NBA.

FOR MORE INFORMATION

Further Reading

Ballard, Chris. *The Art of a Beautiful Game: The Thinking Fan's Tour of the NBA*. New York: Simon & Schuster, 2009.

Bauer, Tom, Greg Hilliard and Kathy Tulumello. *Tough Enough: How the Suns Won the West*. Phoenix Newspapers, Inc., 1993.

Tulumello, Mike. *Breaking the Rules: A Volatile Season with Sports' Most Colorful Team: Charles Barkley's Phoenix Suns*. Longstreet Press, 1996.

Web Links

To learn more about the Phoenix Suns, visit ABDO Publishing Company online at **www.abdopublishing.com**. Web sites about the Suns are featured on our Book Links page. These links are routinely monitored and updated to provide the most current information available.

Places To Visit

Naismith Memorial Basketball Hall of Fame
1000 West Columbus Avenue
Springfield, MA 01105
413-781-6500
www.hoophall.com
This hall of fame and museum highlights the greatest players and moments in the history of basketball. Connie Hawkins and Charles Barkley are among the former Phoenix Suns enshrined here.

US Airways Center
201 East Jefferson Street
Phoenix, AZ 85004
602-379-2000
www.usairwayscenter.com
Originally named America West Arena, this has been the Phoenix Suns' home arena since 1993. The team plays 41 regular-season games here each year.

Wells Fargo Arena
730 Third Street
Des Moines, IA 50309
515-564-8000
www.iowaeventscenter.com
The team headquarters for the Suns' NBA Development League affiliate, the Iowa Energy. Players who are not quite ready for the NBA play in this league.

INDEX

About The Author

Andres "Andy" Ybarra is a Twin Cities-based public relations consultant and freelance sports writer. He spent more than three years as a full-time sports reporter for the Minneapolis bureau of *The Associated Press*, where he covered the Minnesota Timberwolves, Twins, Vikings, and Wild, as well as the University of Minnesota. His work has appeared in several national newspapers and websites. Andy and his wife, Leah, live in Minnesota with their three children.